MY RANDOM MUSINGS

INTERESTING ADVENTURES, STORIES & THOUGHTS FROM MY LIFE

DR. SARBJIT SINGH

(My Parents, Late Dr. Shamsher Singh & Late Mohinder Kaur)

I am dedicating this book to my parents, father Late Dr. Shamsher Singh, and mother Late Mohinder Kaur. My father had a tremendous influence on my life. He was one of the most compassionate people I had ever met or seen. Had a chance to witness this compassion, not just for humans but for every living creature. I shall add some stories from his life, and you'll then understand what I am talking about. He was an eminent eye surgeon of not only the Indian state of Punjab but also of Northern India. I guess he was my inspiration for becoming a doctor (Eye Surgeon).

He was multi-talented. An excellent photographer, he taught me the basics of photography when I was 11 years old or so. He taught me photographic film development in the X-ray dark room in his hospital.

He was a very good violin player, and you would guess, I took up the violin as my instrument of choice for music.

Besides all the above, he showed me what a good human being should be like, what compassion is, and how to always stand by the truth and by those who might need your help.

My mother also had a heart of gold. She was always helping whoever needed help. Shall add a couple of anecdotes about her, too.

I could go on and on about him, but I understand the limitations here and shall, instead, share some anecdotes from his life in this book.

Contents

My Random Musings

Interesting Adventures, Stories & Thoughts from my Life
By Dr. Sarbjit Singh

Copyright & Disclaimer

Disclaimer

Some names, locations, and dates have been changed for privacy reasons.

Edition Information

2nd Edition, 2025

Publisher Information

Dr. Sarbjit Singh #2, SS 1/11 A Kampong Tunku Petaling Jaya 47300 Selangor Malaysia

Author's Website & Socials

?Website: https://sarbjit.in

?YouTube: https://youtube.com/@sarbjitbullepur

Preface

Over the years, life has kept me busy—first with studies, then with medical practice. Yet, in moments of inspiration or reflection, I found solace in writing. Whether it was a thought sparked by an experience or an emotion too profound to ignore, I would put pen to paper, capturing glimpses of my life in words.

For a long time, these writings remained private, shared only with close family and friends. I never considered making them public. But recently, I felt that perhaps, somewhere in the world, someone might find encouragement, inspiration, or even just a moment of joy in these stories. After all, bringing a smile to someone has always been deeply gratifying for me.

These anecdotes, presented without a strict order, are snippets from various chapters of my life. Initially, I thought of including my poetry as well, but I've decided to save those for another book—one that, with the support of readers, I hope to share soon.

I welcome you to these pages, hoping that through my experiences, you find laughter, reflection, and perhaps even a sense of connection.

Acknowledgements

I have to start by thanking my awesome wife, Sharon. From reading early drafts to giving me advice on the whole book to keeping the odd jobs out of my hair so I could edit, she was as important to this book getting done as I was. Thank you so much, dear.

I wrote this book while on vacation in Malaysia, where my wife lives, and I travel up and down from India, where my work is. My daughter, Sherinderjit Kaur, and my son-in-law, Harpal Singh Sandhu, also deserve a big thank you for their moral support and physical support in helping Sharon with the housework, grocery shopping, etc., while I was busy writing.

I would also like to thank my son Shamcharanjit Singh and my daughter-in-law, Dr. Sanya Brar, both of whom are back home in India, taking care of the hospital while I am vacationing in Malaysia. Without their backing and help, I wouldn't have a free mind to write this book.

I would fail in my duty to thank all my patients who have had so much trust in me and have taught me a lot of life lessons.

Sarbjit

An Honor To Share

Dr Sarbjit Singh was awarded 2014 IIRSI Gold Medal for his contribution to Ophthalmology by the Governor of the Indian state of Tamil Nadu. This honour was bestowed during the Annual Conference of Intra-Ocular Implant & Refractive Society of India held in Chennai on 5th & 6th of July 2014.

Humbling Experience

It was an honor to receive a gold medal from IIRSI (Intra-Ocular Implant & Refractive Society of India) in the year 2014 for my work in the field of Ophthalmology. H. E. The Governor of the Indian state of Tamil Nadu gave away the medal.

CHAPTER ONE

A Born Healer: A Childhood Anecdote

My father, the late Dr. Shamsher Singh, was known and loved for his deep compassion toward his patients. His kindness was not something he developed over time—it was inherent in him from childhood. My grandmother once shared an anecdote from his early years, a story that perfectly encapsulates his gentle spirit.

Shamsher and his younger brother, Joginder, were the eldest of ten siblings. They attended the same village school, walking along dusty roads lined with fields of wheat and seasonal crops. Their village was simple—homes built of mud or brick stood on either side of the narrow dirt paths, and beyond them lay stretches of farmland where life moved at a quiet, steady rhythm.

Each day, the brothers walked to school together and returned home side by side. It was routine, unchanging. But one afternoon, something was different—Joginder arrived home alone. Their mother, noticing the unusual absence of her eldest son, immediately grew anxious.

"Joginder, where is Shamsher?" she asked, concern tightening her voice. "Why is he not with you? Is everything alright?"

Joginder hesitated before blurting out, "Bebe, Shamsher has gone mad."

His mother frowned. "Don't speak that way about your elder brother. What do you mean? Tell me exactly what happened."

Joginder sighed and recounted their walk home. "On our way back, we found a dying dog on the dirt road. Shamsher stopped, sat down beside it, and began reciting 'Japji Sahib'—he prayed for the dog to pass peacefully, without suffering."

Silence filled the space between them. Then, without a word, tears welled up in his mother's eyes. Her heart swelled with pride and emotion—her son, so young, already possessed a kindness and empathy far beyond his years.

As Shamsher grew, this innate compassion never faded. He studied medicine, later becoming an eye surgeon, dedicating his life to healing others. His guiding principle remained steadfast, inspired by the sacred teachings of the Sri Guru Granth Sahib ji:

"Service of Man is Service of God."

I Believe

"*I believe that we are just born once. In my mind, there is no afterlife or reincarnation. This is the life we have. Make the most of it. Along the way, just make sure we don't hurt anyone.*"

CHAPTER TWO

"BANGLADESH EYE FLU"

It was probably sometime in 1971, when I was around 12 years old, that there was a very widespread epidemic of eye flu christened Bangladesh Eye Flu. It was probably named so because this was brought in by the huge influx of Bangladeshi refugees into India around the time of the Indo-Pak war. Very infectious, every third or fourth person seemed to be getting it.

At that time, I was studying at a boarding school, Punjab Public School in the erstwhile princely state of Nabha, which was by then a town in the Indian state of Punjab.

As boarders in PPS, there were very few ways of getting away from classes or school. Worse still, probably the only way to be able to go home during regular school days was if we got very sick. This Bangladesh Eye Flu was like a gift from God. Those who were getting 'red eyes' were sent home immediately because of the fear of the spread of the disease.

These kinds of 'gifts', however, have a way of playing hard to get, really hard to get. I and some of my close 'associates' just wouldn't get it no matter how hard we tried. We even tried touching the eyes of the afflicted individuals and then touching our own. Nope, it just wouldn't happen. Damn! What do we do now?

Necessity is the mother of invention, is how that old cliché goes. The 'gang' came up with a cunningly brilliant plan. We would arm ourselves with a bit of toothpaste on one of our fingers each. Go to the MI room (hospital) building. Just before we present ourselves for examination, we would instill that bit of toothpaste into our eyes. It would cause the eyes to go red for just enough time to be diagnosed with the eye flu. We would then get a letter of exemption from school on account of eye flu. Can you beat that? It worked.

Armed with that letter, we went to the housemaster in charge and got permission to go home. I don't quite remember how, but I was on a bus alone to go from Nabha bus station to my destination about 50 km away in Khanna town in the Indian state of Panjab. The journey of the "great escape" began and with a million things going on in my little head, did not take too long to culminate.

The bus guy dropped me off just outside my home. I slowly walked towards the house, both happy and nervous at the same time. As I was walking, I was rehearsing the dialogue that I would deliver to my parents.

When the home door opened, I was told that my parents had gone to a friend's house for dinner. I wasn't sure how long they would take, so I decided to ask someone to drop me off where my parents had gone. I hopped onto the back carrier of the bicycle of an employee of my father's, and we were on our way.

Reaching the place, I rang the doorbell. Ding! Dong!

The domestic help in that house took me into the drawing room where the hosts and my parents were sitting. My parents were surprised beyond belief. Such a thing had never happened that the school kids would be allowed to go home in the middle of a school week.

"How come you are back from school?" asked my father.

"The school people sent me home because I have eye flu," I replied, with some confidence. For a short while, I seemed to have forgotten that my dad was an eye specialist.

"No, you don't!" said my dad, in a harsh voice.

"I wouldn't know," I said meekly as I handed over the letter from the school.

After a brief but tense few moments, my father smiled and hugged me. He was happy that I was with them.

Oh, wait a minute! I suddenly realized that both my parents were wearing dark glasses at night, a sure giveaway that both of them were having eye flu, the great Bangladesh Eye Flu.

Sarbjit SingB-187 (This was my House number at PPS Nabha school)

I Believe

"Using our two hands to act for helping someone is always going to be better than putting those two hands together for prayer."

CHAPTER THREE

SIKHISM: A PATH OF DEVOTION AND EQUALITY

Sikhism is a progressive, forward-thinking religion that emerged in the 15th century CE. Guru Nanak founded it in the region of Panjab, which is now divided between India and Pakistan. At its core, Sikhism is a monotheistic faith, emphasizing devotion to the One God and a life of truth, service, and compassion.

Unlike traditional religious practices that encourage withdrawal from worldly life, Sikhism teaches that spirituality should be practiced by engaging with the world, facing life's challenges, and uplifting others through kindness and integrity.

A Global Faith

Today, Sikhism has a following of over 25 million people worldwide, making it the **fifth-largest religion** globally. Its message of equality, humility, and devotion resonates across cultures, welcoming all who seek a path of righteousness.

Core Teachings

Sikhism advocates:

- Constant remembrance of God in daily life.

- Truthful living with honesty and integrity.

- Equality of all humanity, rejecting discrimination based on caste, race, or gender.

- Service to humankind, promoting generosity and selflessness.

- Denouncement of superstitions and blind rituals, encouraging rational thinking and direct connection with the divine.

The Living Guru: Sri Guru Granth Sahib Ji

Sikhism is rooted in the wisdom of its Ten Gurus, whose teachings are enshrined in the Sri Guru Granth Sahib, the revered Sikh scripture. This sacred text is unique in its inclusivity, incorporating the wisdom of fourteen Hindu saints, such as Ramananda, Kabir, and Namdev, alongside the teachings of one Muslim Sufi saint, Sheikh Farid, symbolizing unity across faiths.

Anticipating challenges in leadership succession, the tenth Sikh Guru, Guru Gobind Singh, made a historic decision: instead of appointing a human successor, he decreed that the Sri Guru Granth Sahib would serve as the eternal Guru of the Sikhs. Since then, Sikhs have honored the Guru Granth Sahib with the same reverence as they would a living Guru, seeking guidance in its divine verses.

The Sikh Place of Worship: Gurdwara

Sikh temples, known as Gurdwaras, embody the faith's principles of openness and inclusivity. Regardless of religion, race, caste, or creed, everyone is welcome in a Gurdwara. Inside, a tradition of selfless service thrives—free vegetarian meals, known as Langar, are served to anyone in need, at any time of the day or night. This practice ensures that no one who enters a Gurdwara leaves hungry, reinforcing the Sikh belief in sharing and serving humanity.

Sikhism is not just a religion; it is a way of life, rooted in love, equality, and selfless service. Its teachings continue to inspire and uplift millions, offering a path of devotion and purpose in an ever-changing world.

A Robert Frost Quote

"In three words I can sum up everything I have learned in life: it goes on"

-Robert Frost

CHAPTER FOUR

DOCTOR-PATIENT RELATIONSHIP

The other day I operated on a patient for cataract removal and intraocular lens implantation. The surgery went quite as usual.

The next morning, the patient came for his first post-operative day checkup.

He: "Doctor, yesterday was the first time that I saw you."

Me: "Is it? The other doctor had seen you before and booked you under me for surgery. But I had gone through your notes a day before your surgery."

He: "Can I say something?"

I prepare myself for a complaint coming my way.

He: "People say that Doctors are only second to God."

I was a bit taken aback and slightly confused about where the conversation was going.

He continues: "Doctor, but I have never seen God. For me, you, who has given me the gift of sight, is God whom I can see."

I could feel my eyes welling up!

There was an uneasy calm. I froze for a second at the enormity of his statement. I was thinking that I don't deserve that high a pedestal, or for that matter, any pedestal.

The only words that came out of my mouth were "Thank you. I am just doing my duty." I gave him a light hug, and he went out of my consulting room quite happy and smiling.

Thoughts about the incident haven't left me ever since. How much trust do the patients put in us? They hand over their lives to us, trusting that we will take care of them and make them better. How can we ever breach that trust? We, as doctors, are blessed immensely in a very unique way to be able to help those who are unwell. We should never forget that. If we keep that in mind all the time that we are dealing with people, especially ones who are sick, we'll never do anything that would jeopardize the pious doctor-patient relationship that we are blessed to be in.

Amen!

Sarbjit Singh

Dr. Shamsher Singh Eye Hospital

Khanna. Punjab. India

Words of Wisdom

*"Surround yourself with people whose eyes light up
and a smile dawns on their face when they see
you."*

CHAPTER FIVE

DOWN WITH GOSSIP

Gossip is talking about people behind their backs or saying something you wouldn't want the other person to hear.

Gossip has a negative connotation to it. Those who gossip about someone do it because, by doing so, they feel superior to the person they are gossiping about.

The person who gossips is someone who carries some resentment towards you and who doesn't have the courage to face you directly and so he found no other option other than talking about you in your absence.

People will gossip about you if they are jealous of you, if they aren't strong enough to face you with their concerns, or if they feel worthless. Those people try to make themselves more worthy by saying that they are better than someone else.

We need to understand that everyone wants to be happy. Sometimes, for a person to feel good about herself or himself, she or he makes others look bad. This is extremely flawed, but it remains one of the ways someone can fool himself or herself into feeling better.

An angry animal is sleeping somewhere deep inside of us, ready to pounce if we come into contact with people who have abused us, quick to growl and thrash at people who let us down in some way.

On a realistic and practical level, this:

- Wastes time.
- Limits empathy.
- Narrows perception.
- Makes us kind of ugly.

If we doubt our integrity or lack faith in ourselves, another person's opinion will matter to us.

By allowing another person's opinion of us to matter so much, we are giving away our strength. This feeling of helplessness bothers us more than the other person's criticism of us. No wonder we feel miserable.

Instead of dwelling on the several people who are bad-mouthing us, we should start focusing on the people who love us, who are there for us, and who will go the extra mile for us. If, for any reason, you feel alone, always remember that you are never alone: you have your inner being with you, and that inner being is always in a state of bliss.

Next time you hear someone bad-mouthing you, just remember that they have no other way of feeling good about themselves, so they have to indulge in bad-mouthing and gossip just to feel good. So allow them to have their moment of joy, and you rejoice in the fact that you are important enough for them to spend time talking about you.

A Mark Twain Quote

*"The only thing worse than being talked about is
not being talked about!"*
- Mark Twain

CHAPTER SIX

HOW TO BUY HAPPINESS

Everyone knows the adage "money can't buy happiness," although very few of us seem to believe it. There is, however, another saying that, "Whoever said money can't buy happiness, isn't spending it right."

Before we learn where to spend it, let us quickly go over some studies.

A study in 2010 by two Nobel Laureates, found that as an individual's income increases, their feeling of well-being increases at a slower and slower rate. After income surpasses about $US 75,000 per year, well-being stops increasing altogether.

Later studies, however, showed that experienced well-being did increase after $US 75000 but at a much slower rate.

We have to keep in mind a simple insight. The more you make, the more you want. The more you have, the less effective it is at bringing you joy and contentment.

"Once you get basic human needs met, a lot more money doesn't make a lot more happiness," notes a psychology professor at Harvard.

So the all-important question is, how do you spend money to buy happiness?

Spending money to have experiences like traveling, learning new things, meeting different people, and exploring different cultures, etc.

Buying time by paying others to do your work. This gives you time to spend with family and friends. It is proven now that the more prosocial you are, the happier you are. So go ahead and spend more time with friends and family.

Now comes what seems to be the most effective way to buy happiness. Giving money away to help others without expecting anything in return, seems to be what gives people the most happiness. So, share with those who are in need, the wealth and resources that you may have to spare.

Founder of Sikhism, Guru Nanak gave Sikhism its three most important tenets.

- Kirat Karo (Earn an Honest Living)
- Naam Japo (Contemplate on God's Name)
- Wand Chhako (Share with others)

So here you have it. Use your money wisely in a way that adds to your happiness and health.

My Quote

" Happiness is a state of mind. We have to consciously work on it"

- Sarbjit

CHAPTER SEVEN

ROOT VERSE (MOOL MANTRA) OF SIKHISM

"Mool Mantra" is the Sikh statement of belief. It means 'basic teaching' or the "Root Verse" and is found at the beginning of every section of the Guru Granth Sahib ji, the religious scripture of the Sikhs. It is repeated each day during early morning prayer.

Its philosophical translation could take hours, and I am not qualified in any way to even attempt that. I shall, however, give you the English translation.

"Ik Onkar" means 'There is only one God'

"Sat Naam" means 'Eternal Truth is his Name'

"Karta Purakh" means 'He is the Creator'

"Nir Bhau" means 'He is without Fear'

"Nir Vair" means 'He is without Enmity'

"Akaal Moorat" means 'He is beyond time and a form which does not exist in time'

"Ajooni" means 'He is beyond Birth and Death'

"Se Bhang" means 'He exists on its own, by its Own'

"Gur Prasaad" means 'He can be reached through the mercy and grace of the true Guru'

ੴ ਸਤਿ ਨਾਮੁ ਕਰਤਾ ਪੁਰਖੁ ਨਿਰਭਉ ਨਿਰਵੈਰੁ ਅਕਾਲ ਮੂਰਤਿ ਅਜੂਨੀ ਸੈਭੰ ਗੁਰ ਪ੍ਰਸਾਦਿ ॥

- एक ओंकार सतनाम, कर्तापुरख, निरिभौ निर्विर, अकाल मूरत, अजूनी सभं. गुरुपरसाद ॥

-Ik-oa'nkār saṯ nām karṯā purakẖ nirbẖa-o nirvair akāl mūraṯ ajūnī saibẖa'n gur parsāḏ.

Tenets Of Sikhism

1. Kirat Karo (Earn an Honest Living)

2. Naam Japo (Contemplate on God's Name)

3. Wand Chhako (Share with others)

- Tenets of Sikhism

CHAPTER EIGHT

COMPASSION TOWARD A PATIENT

This is an anecdote of those days when there were not many eye surgeons around and eye surgeries were not daycare surgeries as they are these days. For example, after cataract surgery, patients stayed in the hospital for five to seven days. Dr. Shamsher Singh's Hospital was a 100-bed hospital, but there were many occasions when the overflow of patients would require extra, temporary tents to be erected on the hospital grounds. Surgery cases were usually kept away from infected cases like those of corneal ulcers.

That day, I had just come back from the hostel, and my father, the late Dr. Shamsher Singh, had just finished with a long surgery list and an even longer outpatient list. He asked my mom and me to stay ready to go to Ludhiana, a big city about 50 km from where we lived. As he was exhausted from work, he wanted to get away from any more work.

We waited in the car as he finished his last couple of cases and sat in the driver's seat. He had driven barely a couple of feet when an oldish-looking man with a stick in hand threw himself on the car bonnet and said, "Doctor, I am having a lot of eye pain. Do something for it."

My dad stopped the car and got out of the car and said to the patient. "I have already seen you and given you treatment. What else do you want me to do? You should go to your bed." I thought it was very unlike him; he seemed a bit harsh on the patient. He was probably finished with his patience after such a long, tiring day, or so we thought. Later, I realized that this was out of frustration and helplessness in mitigating the patient's distress. The old man got to one side. My dad sat in the car, and we were on our way.

No one spoke a word for about a couple of miles. Then suddenly my dad stopped the car and turned it around, and we were back home, which was on the hospital premises. Still, no words, and he got out of the car and walked towards the hospital. I followed him just a few steps behind.

After a while, I found myself in a tent where corneal ulcer patients were admitted. He looked for that old man who was in pain. The old man was lying on a bed with his arm wrapped around his eyes and face. My dad sat on his bedside and spoke. "Baba ji (respected elder), is the pain really bad? I have already given you all the medicines I could. The only other thing I can do for you right now is to massage your head. Let me do it for you." I stood at the foot end of the bed over the next fifteen minutes or so, witness to something that I would carry with me throughout my life.

Sarbjit

Love

Spread Love, Not Hatred

CHAPTER NINE

My Kids Showed They Have Compassion

Dr. Sanya Brar (my daughter-in-law): "Dad, there is an old man who needs an OCT investigation for his retinal disease. It will cost him ₹1800/~. He is very poor and can't afford it. I have decided to pay for him."

Me: "That's a good gesture, but we do have a charitable trust that can pay for him."

Shamcharanjit Singh (my son), with tears in his eyes: "Dad, the old man earns only ₹2250/~ a month. His kids don't care for him. If he pays that much, how will he survive the rest of the month? He may need another ₹ 7000/- for treatment. I have arranged a donor who is willing to chip in. The remaining I will pay."

This little conversation reassured my heart that compassion and kindness are very much alive and kicking in these kids.

These kids won't let any patient go away from Dr. Shamsher Singh Eye Hospital for lack of finances.

Sarbjit Singh

A Mark Twain Quote

*"Compassion is the language the blind can see and
the deaf can hear."*
— Mark Twain

CHAPTER TEN

THE RAT AND ME

I sat at the edge of the bed with one leg dangling, busy playing with my new iPhone, unmindful of the unpleasant experience that I was going to encounter.

I was startled by a sudden movement of something on my still-dangling leg. As if by reflex, my hand, with all the energy and quickness, went down to grab my thigh. I suddenly realized that a small little brat rat had ventured into my pajamas and was going up towards the forbidden area. What nerve and balls does this rat have? No, no, buddy. This is a no-entry zone.

I jumped and shook my leg and the whole body as if being electrocuted. Before I knew it, the rat had beaten a retreat and run under the bed. I took my flip-flop, the only potential weapon that I had near me, and banged it against the bed and on the floor, trying to scare the rat out. No, the rat wasn't coming out.

It took me a bit to realize how close to a disaster I had been. I felt insulted. I felt angry. I felt violated. This rat was not getting away with it.

In a huff and a puff, I went out of my room looking for a rat trap with ammo, a small piece of bread. It was war. The room had been mined. I lay on my bed with the lights off, but my senses were all heightened and waiting for the enemy to make a move. No movement. No sound. I waited and waited. I didn't even realize when I fell asleep.

I was rudely awakened by a sudden snapping sound. The mine had gone off. The enemy had been captured. I felt vindicated, and I felt powerful. I looked at the rat with contempt, but the rat was a rat and kept moving around in the trap as if looking for an escape route.

The culprit had been caught. I was its victim and also the only eyewitness. My wife took the honorary positions of judge, jury, and executioner. This guy had no chance of escape or mercy. The verdict was as expected, and the sentencing was swift.

"To be drowned till death."

Sarbjit

About The Author

Dr. Sarbjit Singh

Dr. Sarbjit Singh is an ophthalmologist by profession. He has been doing that since 1984. His life has been dedicated to his profession, but he occasionally does find time for writing short articles, poetry, and stories, mostly inspired by real-life incidents.

He is an ardent amateur photographer, singer, violin player, music composer, and YouTuber.

https://www.youtube.com/@sarbjitbullepur
https://dsseh.com
https://sarbjit.in

www.ingramcontent.com/pod-product-compliance
Lightning Source LLC
Chambersburg PA
CBHW020513160726
47991CB00007B/2939